ANN MORRIS

◆◆

LOVING

PHOTOGRAPHS BY KEN HEYMAN

A MULBERRY PAPERBACK BOOK
NEW YORK

First Mulberry Edition, 1994

5 7 9 10 8 6 4

ISBN 0-688-13613-3

The Library of Congress has cataloged the Lothrop, Lee & Shepard edition of *Loving* as follows:
Morris, Ann.
    Loving / by Ann Morris; photographs by Ken Heyman.
        p.   cm.   Summary: Provides examples of the different ways in which love can be expressed, with an emphasis on the relationship between parent and child.
    1. Parent and child—Juvenile literature 2. Love—Juvenile literature.
    [1. Love. 2. Parent and child.] I. Heyman, Ken, ill. II. Title.
    HQ755.85. M66 1990   306 . 7—dc20   90-33844
                                                                                    CIP AC

LOVING

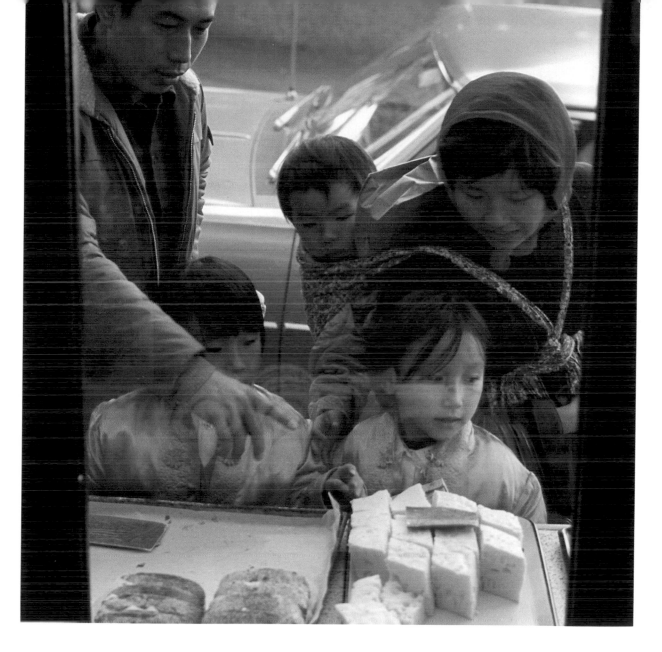

Mommies and daddies
take care of you for a long time.

They give you food

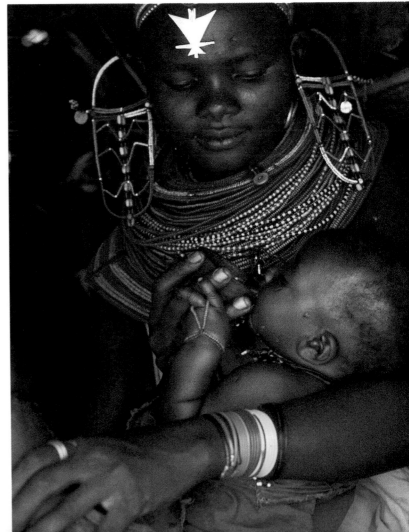

and keep you clean and tidy.

10   They make sure you are dressed and cozy.

They listen to what you have to say.
They tell you stories and tuck you in at bedtime. 11

They take you
to the market

and for walks
and talks.

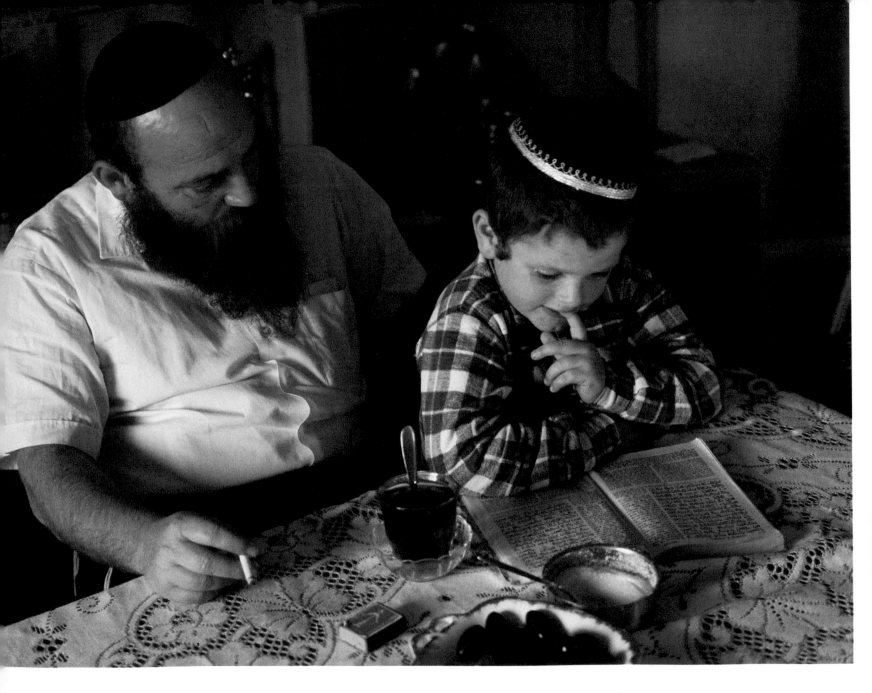

14   They teach you to read

and to count...

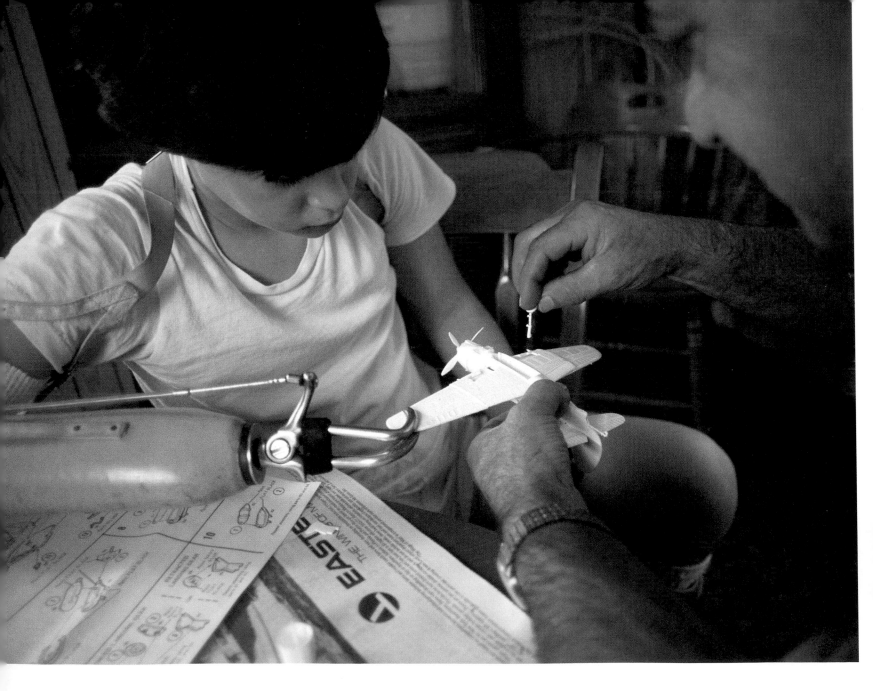

16   to build a plane...

to sew.

18   They teach you how to ride a pony

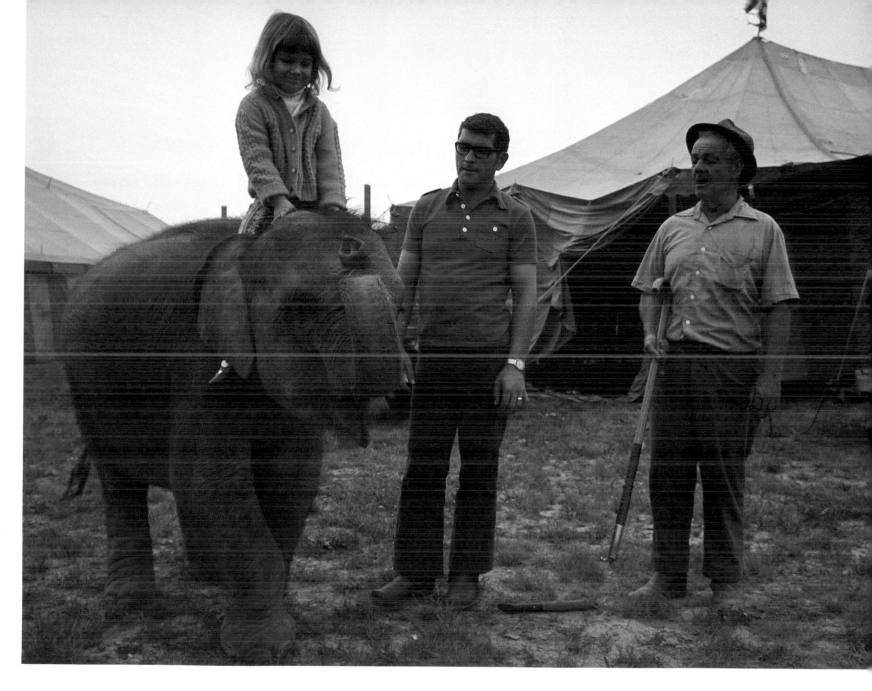

and even how to ride an elephant! 19

Older children
help younger children.

Good friends share good times together.

Children play with their pets

and care for them
in loving ways.

27

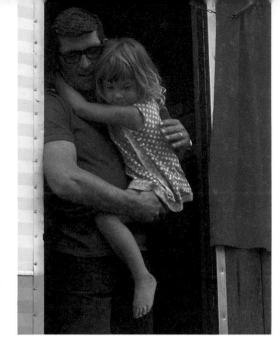

Daddies hug
and cuddle.

Even elephants
snuggle.

28

And mommies kiss and smile and open their arms.

INDEX

16 UNITED STATES: A mechanical arm helps this boy, who lost his real arm in an injury, build a plane with his father.

17 UNITED STATES: This Hispanic girl lives in Brooklyn, New York. Her mother sews at home to earn extra money for the family.

18 UNITED STATES: Learning to ride a pony is important to this Navajo boy. In addition to the pony, his family has four horses and two dozen sheep.

19 UNITED STATES: This little girl's family is part of a traveling circus.

20 UNITED STATES: This father and son are enjoying their day in New York City.

21 UNITED STATES: Ordinarily, this Navajo father wears his yellow bandana only on Sundays when he goes to tribal meetings.

22 UNITED STATES: Rolling in the autumn leaves is fun. This family lives in a suburb of Chicago.

23 UNITED STATES: Sometimes sharing is hard.

23 INDIA: This Sikh father is a photographer. You can tell he is a proper Sikh by his name (Singh), his beard, his turban, and the bracelet he wears on his wrist.

24 JAPAN: This little girl wears an obi, which is a kind of sash, around her kimono.

24 HONG KONG: The older child is a kind of child nurse. She has been taught how to take care of the younger children in her family while their parents are at work.

25 UNITED STATES: These boys are trying to catch catfish in a stream. They are using casting plugs to lure the fish.

26 UNITED STATES: This Navajo boy is sitting inside his hogan. A hogan is a round house with a center pole and a hole in the roof to let out smoke from a wood-burning fire.

27 UNITED STATES: These boys have a pet rabbit.

27 UNITED STATES: These children live in a trailer, which moves from place to place with the traveling circus.

28 UNITED STATES: The elephants are chained to a post so they won't wander off. They use their trunks the way people use their arms—for eating, picking things up, and for loving.

Where in the world were these photographs taken?

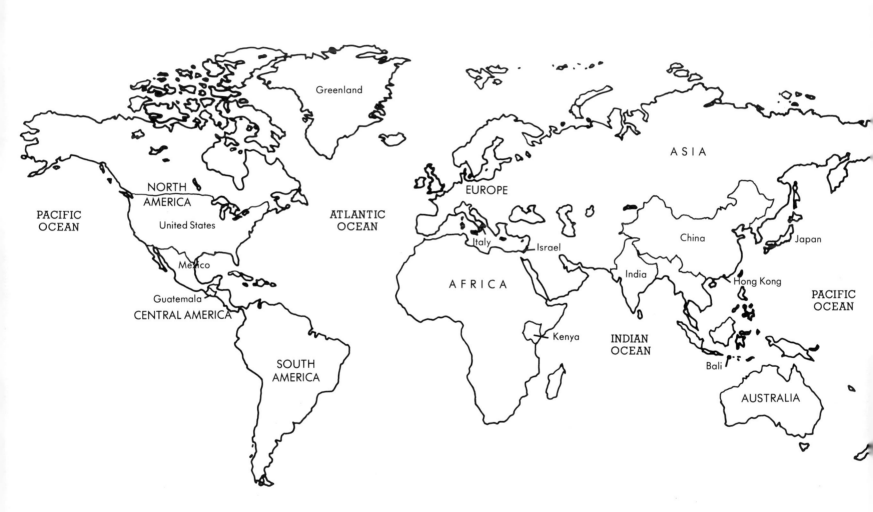

PACIFIC OCEAN

NORTH AMERICA

United States

Mexico

Guatemala

CENTRAL AMERICA

SOUTH AMERICA

Greenland

ATLANTIC OCEAN

EUROPE

AFRICA

ASIA

Italy

Israel

Kenya

India

China

Japan

Hong Kong

INDIAN OCEAN

Bali

PACIFIC OCEAN

AUSTRALIA